Leadership Strategies in Organizations

Theories and approaches to preparing the leader manager

Era of Modern Management

HR. Sustainable Development

Ibrahim H. Hussney

Accredited Lecturer and Instructor

© Intellectual Property Rights

All rights reserved to the author, and this book may not be exchanged in whole or in part illegally; whether by making it available for downloading on websites or exchanging it via e-mail messages, no part of the text may be copied without its prior permission.

"Investing in building human beings is now at the top of the pyramid of states' concerns as the most important industry in this information age, as a result of nations realizing that their fate and future will always depend on the creativity of their citizens, and the extent of their challenge and response towards change always for the better....!!!!"

CONTENTS

Introduction...
What is leadership?

The current era witnessed many successive technological and knowledge developments, which had a role in finding modern ways of leadership in business organizations and how to develop them. Leadership is an art, ingenuity, and talent, and it is one of the strategic roles of managers, in which the value and merit of leadership prowess vary among managers.

Some acquire it by personal instinct for their own sake, while others are present in it by virtue of their position. Still, they do not have control over their affairs, which obliges all administrative and business organizations to find creative leaders with innovative methods and quick organizational solutions.

The transformational leadership style has been one of the most important leadership styles produced by scientific progress and technical development, due to its high ability to lead business and face modern challenges and developments by influencing the behavior of subordinates, developing their creative abilities, and encouraging them to face problems and difficulties facing work.

The self represents the first step on the ladder of career success, and since governmental organizations need more than others a transformational leadership style that can detonate the latent energies of the employees working in them, and provide them with the opportunity to search for new things in the field of work and the continuous modernization of work systems in accordance with the changes surrounding all countries.

The concept of leadership in general is one of the concepts that attracts the attention of researchers in the field of management. Leadership does not necessarily mean occupying important job positions in business organizations only but rather means the ability to persuade and influence others, which requires that administrative leadership have the characteristics and skills that enable it to perform the leadership role effectively and efficiently, whether inside or outside the work environment, and the completion of these works in their entirety with great skill, and comes at the forefront of planning, organizing, coordinating and decision-making and. leadership requirements manifest in the ability to persuade and influence others.

If we want to shorten the words in order to express what leadership is, then we can say that leadership is the ability to influence individuals in order to stimulate their desire towards achieving the goals that all people seek to achieve, and if we touch on institutional work, in this case, leadership is considered as the link between workers and between the organization's plans and future visions, as it works to unify the efforts of workers towards achieving the set goals, and allows control of work problems, and draws the necessary plans to solve them, as well as develops, trains, cares and motivates individuals, In addition to increasing their self-capacity and improving their humanitarian and practical skills.

Your success or failure as a manager will certainly depend on the leadership qualities that you enjoy, without which you cannot generate the possibility of being a successful leader by helping your subordinates to find solutions to their practical and humanitarian problems alike.

You are involved with all the resources of the organization, the business enterprise, or the company, in drawing and formulating strategies, organizing and monitoring activities in order to achieve the goals, choosing the appropriate ones from the organization's purposes and objectives, and in making possible decisions for what needs to be done and motivating people to do so.

Thus, leadership is the function of management that is largely involved in setting goals and motivating people to help achieve them. One of the most important things that leaders do is set and define goals that the organization, business enterprise, or company wants to become a reality, and help subordinates and guide them on the right way to achieve these goals.

It is possible for a person to be an effective manager, a good planner, and an organized administrator, but at the same time lacks the motivational skills that a leader should have, to direct the energy required to stimulate and motivate subordinates in the organization, business enterprise, or company.

Due to the complexity of business in organizations today towards managing them with the required speed and image through sound decision-making, and in order to raise the level of effective participation of all employees, the choices of most organizations, businesses, projects, and companies today focus on bringing in managers who possess the required leadership skills.

Since the issue of leadership has the main and fundamental role in the institutional change in business organizations as an abstract phenomenon characterized by ambiguity, administrative leaders have been able to transform the goals related to the people they subordinate to a reality called the ability to create and highlight talents and their influence on those around them, and from here leadership can be defined in the framework of administrative work, as the process by which employees or workers can be influenced and persuaded to work in order to achieve the goals of the organization efficiently and effectively.

Chapter one...
Concept and definition of
leadership in organizations

Harold Koontz and *Heinz Weinrich* define leadership as ***"the art or process of influencing people to strive enthusiastically toward group goals"***. In other words, leadership is the ability to persuade others to work toward achieving goals.

In other words, leadership is the ability to persuade others to work towards achieving specific goals with enthusiasm, that is, in the end, it is the human factor that binds a group together and motivates them towards achieving goals, and this is the work of leaders towards helping the group achieve goals through the optimal use of its capabilities.

Based on the previous definition, some leadership features can be identified as follows:

• Leadership is a process through which the ability to influence others is exercised.

• Leadership is the use of non-coercive influence toward shaping the goals of a group or organization and motivating behavior toward achieving those goals.

• Leadership involves authority and responsibility, in terms of deciding the course of the road, and taking responsibility for the success or failure towards achieving the goals that have been agreed upon.

• Leadership must include other people within the organization, business institution, or company, such as employees and professionals, who help with their willingness to accept the trend toward determining the status of the leader's influence.

• Leadership must involve an unequal distribution of power between leaders and a group of individuals, knowing that group members are not as powerless as some think, they can engage and activate group activities in many directions, however, the leader is usually more powerful.

• The principle of leadership includes the application of certain values, as leadership based on ethical principles needs to give followers the required knowledge and sufficient alternatives in order to make smart choices when it comes to responding to the leader's suggestions.

Ways to develop leaders to become more effective

Experience has shown that the keys to the success of the organization, business enterprise, or company always refer to the inevitability of managers who are able to inspire subordinates in order to obtain a very distinguished performance.

Because of this reason, many researchers resorted to in order to arrive at the description of the "good manager", so that it is possible to identify the desired traits in a person in order to be a good manager and measure that, and this research has concluded that the following methods are used to reach the best performance of the manager's subordinates:

1- Proper use of management in accordance with the achievement of objectives

Proper management in accordance with the achievement of goals is an effective technique through which specific goals are set that may find it difficult to achieve, and here it is the responsibility of managers to work on directing subordinates towards the right direction in order to overcome the difficulties that prevent the achievement of those goals.

2- Provide meaningful and interesting work for subordinates

It is always noted that subordinates have an inherent desire to accomplish the work. Accordingly, the good manager must seize this opportunity in order to provide work for the subordinates that may arouse interest and be characterized by a spirit of challenge.

When subordinates gain experience and become qualified in their work, they should be given higher responsibilities, and not be absent from the mind of a good manager to provide the principle of incentives and rewards to raise the level of their excitement towards the completion of the work in the best way possible.

3- Focus on communication and contact skills

Communication between different departments in the organization, business enterprise, or company, and communication between individuals, are two of the most important factors that work to facilitate and complete the vocabulary of the work wheel.

The successful manager is one who seeks to remove all major barriers that prevent effective communication, where he must be in constant and clear contact with his subordinates, especially when giving specific instructions, and the leader manager must not only be able to communicate well but must also be a good listener, in order to be able to understand the concerns of individuals and the possibility of addressing them in appropriate ways.

A good manager must also anticipate other important aspects related to communication, with regard to giving the required care and attention to the different reactions of subordinates, and he must also communicate his reaction clearly to the subordinates about the work they are doing so that they can improve their level of performance.

4- Resorting to the use of effective evaluation of subordinates

A good manager who is characterized by the spirit of leadership must determine and measure the level of performance of the subordinate, and this can be reached by comparing the actual performance with the desired results to be reached, and the rewards must be monitored,

And let this is related to the degree of performance evaluation while working to enhance the effective performance of subordinates, and this evaluation must be used to shed light also on areas of interest related to work management, and he also has the responsibility to show subordinates how required to improve their performance.

5- Proper delegation of authority and responsibility

The leader manager should give sufficient and correct authority and responsibility to the subordinates to perform a specific task, which raises the level of motivation towards the outstanding achievement of the work of the subordinates if they are given greater responsibilities or tasks.

6- Teamwork building

Capable and effective teamwork is a good manager's tool for accomplishing business and achieving goals according to the strategies that are set in advance for the organization, business enterprise, or company, and therefore the manager must ensure that each subordinate understands his role, and is aware of the responsibilities entrusted to him, notify his subordinates that they are part of the larger team that includes all members of the organization, business enterprise, or company.

The manager must also inform his subordinates of the tasks and activities carried out by the organization, business enterprise, or company, and make them feel the importance of their effective contribution towards achieving the required profits.

7- Resorting to the use of unified procedures for decision-making

The leader manager must ensure that the decisions that are taken have a required entitlement, are implemented within a specific time frame, and are accepted by the subordinates, and for that, he must design specific procedures, with objective and unified criteria, according to the nature of the issue in order to make the right relating decision, which entails taking its executive measures.

Chapter two …
Main elements of leadership
in organizations

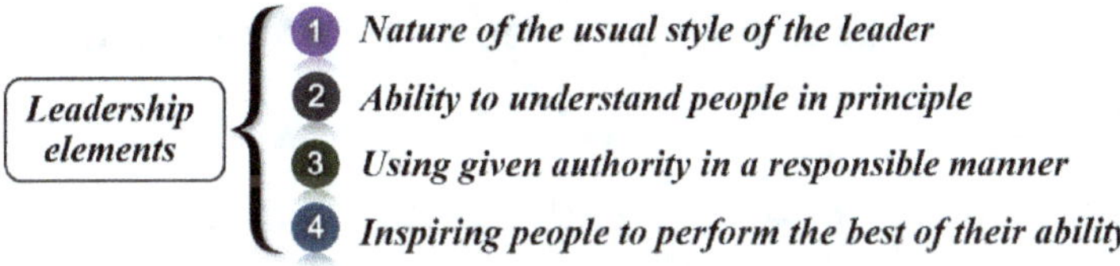

In order for any group of individuals to perform its duties effectively and achieve its goals, it must have a leader who guides it to the right path and supports it with his ideas and decisions. This leader must have these four elements:

1 - The ability to inspire team members of subordinates.

2- The ability to use energy reserves effectively and responsibly.

3- The ability to act in a way that harmoniously develops the work culture.

4- The ability to understand the fact that people are motivated by different forces, at different times, and in different situations.

Developing leaders at Infosys
(case study)

The founders of Infosys Information Systems wanted to build an organization that would survive and could function even under uncertain conditions, and with this in mind, the Chairman of the Board of Directors of the company, Narayana N. R. Murthy, has established an advisory body known as the Board of Directors charged with making strategic decisions for the company,

Narayana had noticed that during the meetings of the aforementioned board of directors, the young workers of the company were reluctant to submit proposals, and Narayana conducted further research on this subject, he found that these young employees have many good ideas, but are reluctant to contribute to discussions due to fear arising from intimidation by their superiors.

This phenomenon disturbs Narayana, who as a result decides to construct an institute of leadership, which will promisingly help employees at all level to eventually develop them into leaders.

The Infosys Leadership Institute (ILI) was established in 2001, with the aim of responding to the following specific challenges:

• Helping employees manage the huge and steady growth of the company.

• Creating greater value for customers through what is called *"thought leadership"*.

• To prepare Infosys employees to be always ready to face the complexities of the market and the variables of the dynamic external environment.

Through our study of this case, we were able to show that Infosys considers the issue of preparing leaders from managers as a journey that starts from the stage of selecting high-potential employees, where they are selected and determined by senior management from among a group of candidates based on their previous level of performance, as well they are evaluated in terms of their ability to lead. And each employee with high potential will be assigned a faculty by the Infosys Institute for leaders, provided that the faculty members direct these employees by setting personal development plans (PDPs)), in addition to developing business management plans for these employees.

Potential employees will also be trained on more than one leadership skill, and this training within this institute may take three years until the employee becomes an effective leader.

Infosys model for the nine pillars of leadership development

Infosys Information Systems took the lead in constructing this model, which aims to enhance and develop the leadership skills of its employees. This model was developed after carefully analyzing the highly successful operations followed by 18 other international companies.

The success of these companies' operations is due to the fact that each pillar in this model has a unique importance that develops individual leadership competencies, where the employee can choose one or more of these pillars for his self-development, however, the starting point is always the first basic pillar which is called "***the degree of reaction estimated at 360 degrees***." as for participation in other areas contained in the pillars, it becomes optional and depends on the employee himself. These nine pillars are:

1- Practical learning.

2- Development tasks.

3- Community sympathy.

4- Leadership skills training.

5- Systematic learning process.

6- Development of relationships.

7- Intensive programs for reactions.

8- Workshops to teach the culture of Infosys.

9- The degree of reaction is estimated at 360 degrees.

Speaking of the first pillar, which is called the "360 Degree of Reaction," which is referred to the way in which systematic data about a person's performance and abilities are collected from many co-workers, including colleagues, direct observers, managers, and internal and external customers, provided that the feedback represented in the data obtained is used to prepare self-development plans for individuals, as this comes in order to enhance their current skills and provide them with more new skills through following up on the teaching staff at the Infosys Institute for Leaders.

Elements of leadership in organizations

The elements of leadership include four main headings:

1- *Using the granted power in a responsible manner*, where power is defined as the control imposed on others, or in other words, it is the ability to influence the behavior of others, hence the leaders in organizations usually depend on some or all of the main bases of power.

2- *The ability to understand people in principle*, because once the motivational theories are understood, the types of motivational forces, and the nature of the motivational system, are not considered sufficient, as the leader must also be able to apply this knowledge to people in different situations.

If he is able to understand the elements of motivation, he will have the ability to focus his awareness more on the nature and strengths associated with human needs, which will help him find ways to meet these needs in order to eventually obtain the desired results from them.

3- *Inspiring people to perform tasks to the best of their ability*, and this inspiration indicates that, in addition to the old employees who assume the position of chiefs, they can have what inspires subordinates through various incentives, but the behavior of these chiefs in itself is considered as a motivating force weighty.

Another thing of influence is the charismatic and personal nature of the leader which gives birth to loyalty, sincerity, and a strong desire on the part of the subordinates to carry out the instructions. In such cases, the subordinates do not just try to meet their own needs but they will give unconditional support to the leader, the owner of this charisma.

4- *The nature of the usual style of the leader*, in this regard, we can say that there is no doubt that the usual style that the leader adopts will have an impact on the work climate in the group of subordinates, organization, business enterprise, or company because the motivational force of the leader's followers must have and be affected by what is expected of him, and also by perceived rewards, tasks to be performed, and other factors that are part of the work climate in the organization or business enterprise, or the company.

We cannot deny that leadership behavior always has a great influence on these factors, which in turn affect the work climate, and therefore a lot of research has been conducted in this field so that many management scholars consider that good leadership is a result of the appreciation of psychology towards personal relationships, it should also be noted that the most important job of good managers is to design the environment that will help the organization, business enterprise, or company achieve its goals and provide ways to maintain them.

A good leader manager must try to push the work of each member in general of the subordinates in the entity to be more productive and to be satisfactory, and this will only come by working to understand the underlying motives of these subordinates, such as their job status, the authority vested in them, and the money earned "***wages***", a sense of pride as a result of doing the work, etc., and do not forget the works of the leader to fulfill them.

In simple words, the basic principle of leadership can be described as "***Since people tend to follow those who, in their opinion, offer them the means to achieve their personal goals, the more managers understand what motivates their subordinates and how these motivators work, and the greater the understanding these managers have towards implementing this through their managerial procedures, the greater the weighting effect towards them to become leaders***".

Chapter three ...
Leadership theories and their development

Attempts to explain and understand the essence of leadership has led to the formulation of various leadership theories. Research in this field has reached four theories of leadership. They are trait theory, behavior theory, situational theory (contingency theory), and finally transformational theory.

Leadership traits theory

In the 40s, of the last century most of the early leadership studies focused on attempting to identify the traits of a leader, due to that, the trait theory was born as a result of the first systematic effort by psychologists and other researchers to understand leadership. This theory saw that leaders share certain passive and inactive personality traits.

The first theory in this context was what is called the "great man theory", which actually dates back to the era of the ancient Greeks and Romans. According to this theory, leaders are born and not made, and many researchers have tried to identify the physical, mental, and personal characteristics of the various leaders. However, the great man theory lost much of its momentum and relevance with the rise of the behaviorist school of psychology.

Ralph M. Stogdill, in his survey of leadership theories and research, found that many researchers have linked some specific traits to leadership ability, including physical traits ***(such as appearance, energy, and height)***, four traits ***(including intelligence and ability)***, and sixteen personality traits ***(including ability adaptability, enthusiasm, aggressiveness, and self-confidence)***, six task-related traits ***(including achievement, orientation, initiative, and perseverance)***, and nine social traits ***(including interpersonal skills, cooperation, and managerial ability)***.

More recently, researchers have identified key leadership traits as ***leadership motivation (that is, the desire to lead in the absence of a thirst for power), directiveness (such as achievement, energy, ambition, initiative, and perseverance), honesty and integrity, self-confidence including emotional stability, and ability, perceptual, understanding, and comprehension of business***.

In general, studying leadership in terms of traits has not been a very successful approach to explaining what leadership is, because not all leaders possess all the traits mentioned in this theory, while many non-leaders possess many of them, moreover, the trait approach does not give a definitive estimate of how many of these traits a potential leader might have.

Here we can say that the various studies on leadership traits do not all agree on defining these traits, or how they relate to leadership behavior, as most of these traits are in fact, patterns of human behavior.

Behavioral theories

When it became clear that effective leaders did not seem to have a particular set of distinguishing features, researchers tried to study the behavioral aspects of these effective leaders. In other words, rather than trying to figure out who the effective leaders are.

The researchers tried to find out and define what this type of leader does, how they delegate tasks, how they communicate with them and try to motivate those who follow them or subordinates, how they carry out their tasks, and so on.

The course of this research has taken a lot of work largely at **the University of Iowa, the University of Michigan, and Ohio State University**.

Leadership behaviors

Kurt Lewin, a researcher at the **University of Iowa**, and his colleagues made some early attempts to define effective leadership behaviors scientifically, as they focused on three leadership styles, namely, **authoritarianism, democracy, and the principle of non-interference in the affairs of others**, and the result indicated that **the authoritarian leader** tends to make decisions without involving subordinates, clarifies work methods, and provides workers with very limited knowledge of goals, and sometimes gives negative feedback.

While **the democratic leader** calls for the group's participation in decision-making, he consults with subordinates on proposed actions and encourages them. Democratic leaders allow the group to define work methods, make overarching goals known, and use feedback to assist subordinates.

As for ***the leader who adheres to the principle of non-interference in the affairs of others***, he rarely uses his authority, and he allows his group of subordinate's complete freedom to undertake actions under his direction.

Despite the difference in these leadership doctrines, these leaders depend to a large extent on their subordinates to determine their own goals and ways to achieve them.

These leaders see that their role is limited to assisting the completion of work related to their subordinates, by providing them with information, and acting primarily as a contact with the external environment for this group of subordinates, and these leaders often avoid giving responses to reactions.

In order to determine the most effective leadership style, Lewin and his colleagues trained some people to display each of these styles separately, and then put them in charge of different groups in a pre-teen boys' club, and the result of this research training indicated that the groups headed by the leader who believes in the principle of non-interference in the affairs of others who are underperforming compared to other groups headed by authoritarian leaders and others who are democrats.

It was also found that the amount of work performed was equal in groups with authoritarian and democratic leaders, the quality of work and group satisfaction was higher in the democratic groups, and, it was also shown from the research that the performance of democratic leadership led to both good quantity and quality of work, and an impression of comfort among workers.

However, later research showed that democratic leadership sometimes showed higher performance than authoritarian leadership, but at other times led to a performance that was lower than or equal to performance under the authoritarian style, while it seems that the democratic leadership style makes subordinates more satisfied, it did not always lead to higher or even equal performance, which put the managers in a dilemma towards choosing the optimal style of leadership, moreover, and as a given fact not used by many managers the democratic method at work. .

In order to make it easier to choose the required leadership style, **Robert Tannenbaum and Warren H. Schmidt**, an acclaimed management scholar, has designed a continuum of leadership behaviors, as shown in the following illustration:

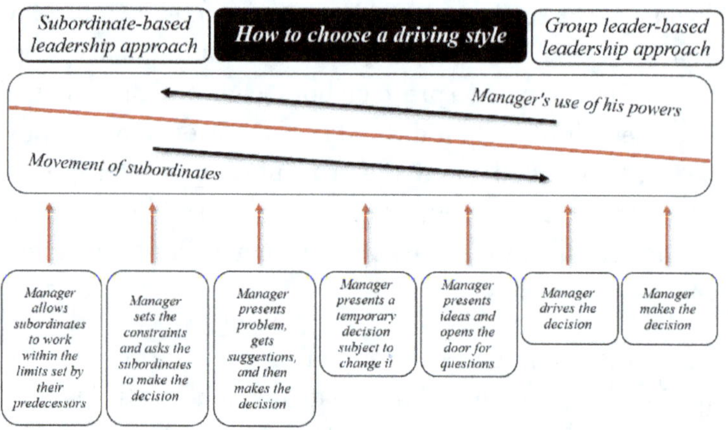

This continuum presents a vision of different degrees of leadership behavior, ranging from the approach based on the head of a group on the far right (the leader) to the approach based on subordinates on the far left. It may be noted here that moving away from the end of the authoritarian approach in this continuum represents a step towards the beginning of the democratic approach and vice versa.

According to Tannenbaum and Schmidt, when a decision is made to select an appropriate leadership style, the person in the position of manager *(leader)* must consider his or her own strength *(such as level of comfort with different alternatives)*, the situation *(such as time pressures)*, and within subordinates *(such as willingness to take responsibility)*.

The researchers involved in this study suggested that in the short term, depending on the situation, the leader should exercise some flexibility in his behavior, the leader should create the ability to improve decision quality, encourage teamwork, motivate employees, raise morale, and develop employee performance.

Further work on leadership at **the University of Michigan** seems to confirm that an employee-centered approach appears to be much more beneficial compared to a work-focused approach, or a production-focused approach.

In an employee-centered approach, leaders focus on building effective work teams committed to high performance, while In the work-focused approach, work is broken down into routine tasks, and leaders monitor workers closely to ensure that prescribed methods are followed and productivity standards are met.

Here we should point out that there are still differences in the level of feedback resulting from this study, sometimes the work-focused approach produced higher feedback compared to the employee-focused approach, therefore, no specific conclusions can be drawn, and it seems necessary to conduct more studies and research on this topic.

In 1945, a group of researchers at **Ohio University** began extensive investigations about leadership, as they engaged in a research process in order to identify a number of important leadership behaviors, through which the researchers designed a questionnaire to measure the behaviors of various leaders and track some factors such as group performance and satisfaction to find out which behaviors are of most effectiveness, and the most prevalent aspect of the studies was the identification of two dimensions of leadership behavior, namely, the *"starting structure"* and *"considerations"*.

The starting structure is the extent to which a leader defines his or her role or that of subordinates in order to achieve organizational goals, a role similar to the job-focused leader behavior in the Michigan studies, but includes a broader set of managerial functions such as planning, organizing, directing, and focuses mainly on task-related issues.

As for *the considerations*, they reflect the degree of mutual trust between the leader and his subordinates, and to what extent the leader respects the ideas of subordinates, and shows some concern for their feelings.

Similar to the behavior of the employee-centered leader in the Michigan studies, that is, focusing on people issues, the consideration-oriented leader is more likely to be friendly toward subordinates, encourage participation in decision-making, and maintain two-way communication.

In contrast to the Iowa and Michigan studies, which consider the dimensions of leadership, i.e., the employee-centered approach, and the work-focused approach, as opposite ends of the same continuum, the Ohio studies considered starting to create a structure and considering two independent behaviors, therefore, leadership behaviors operate on separate links, and thus the leader can be higher in each of the dimensions, or higher in one dimension and lower in another dimension, or can resort to gradation between dimensions, this two-dimensional pattern in the behavior of the leader made sense as with many leaders, he offered both starting structure and considerations.

This two-dimensional pattern was designed by researchers at Ohio University, which can be seen in the following illustration:

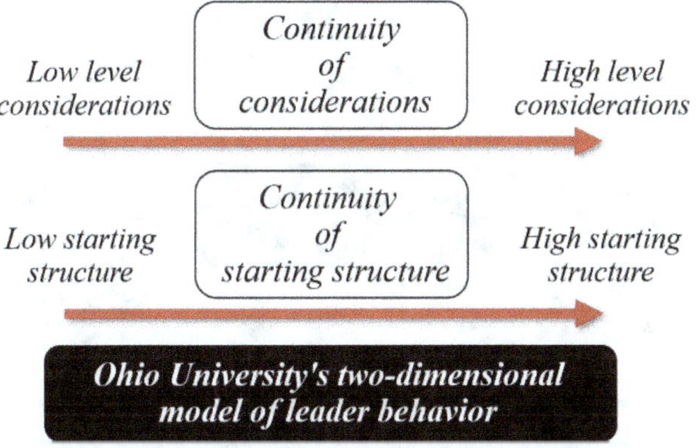

The two-dimensional approach has given birth to an interesting possibility. As a leader, you will be able to focus on both tasks and people-related issues. You will also be able to produce high levels of satisfaction in subordinates by activating considerations, and at the same time, expected results can be defined, and thus focus on important topics as well.

This theory was so simple that it became clear that situational factors such as the nature of the task and the expectations of subordinates must influence the success of leadership behavior.

Likert's four systems of management

Professor Rensis Likert and his associates at ***the University of Michigan*** have studied patterns and methods of leaders and managers over three decades, and have developed specific ideas and approaches to understanding leadership behavior, in order to keep all departments or personnel working in unison, he, therefore, proposed four systems of management.

Reliable exploitative style of leadership

The style of this system represents the behavior of dictatorial leadership, in all decisions taken by managers, with a decrease in the participation of employees, and these managers are predominantly authoritarian, have no confidence in their subordinates, and resort to the use of negative motivational tactics such as intimidation and punishment, and retain decision-making powers with them only.

The reliable utility style of leadership

In contrast to the method of the first administrative system represented by the method of reliable exploitation, the managers, by following the method of this system, have complete care of overall business issues, and at the same time, they have confidence in their subordinates.

They also allow vertical communication to a certain level by subordinates, and always demand their participation. Under this managerial style, managers use reward and punishment systems in order to motivate workers. They allow subordinates to participate to some extent in decision-making but maintain close control over policies.

Consultative leadership style

Managers under the method of this system do not have confidence and reassurance towards subordinates, and despite that, they always seek advice from subordinates, while preserving the right to make the final decision, and this administrative method includes:

1- Motivating employees with rewards and punishment sometimes.

2- Resorting to the flow of vertical communication from top to bottom and vice versa.

3- Managers work as consultants in order to solve the various problems that the work wheel is exposed to.

4- What is related to public policy and crucial decisions, it is the one that is taken by the higher levels of management, while other specific decisions are taken by other lower levels of management.

Participatory leadership style

Managers who follow the method of this system give full confidence in their subordinates and their abilities, and they always ask about the opinions of subordinates and use those opinions constructively, and they encourage the participation of employees at all levels towards decision-making.

Vertical communication is resorted to from top to bottom and vice versa, and managers under this system deliberately work in a team spirit with their subordinates and with other managers, and through this system also the participation of employees towards achieving goals is crowned with financial rewards.

Likert found that those managers who adopted this approach had the greatest success as leaders, as they were more effective in setting goals and achieving them, and were more productive in general. This research concluded that high productivity is always associated with the third and fourth management systems when both the first and second systems are characterized by low productivity.

Administrative leadership network

The Administrative Leadership Network, designed by **Robert Blake and Jane Srygley Mouton**, is a popular approach in which different leadership styles are identified.

They consider managerial behavior to be a function of two variables, caring for people and caring production, and that this management network can be seen as a framework to help managers determine their leadership style and rationalize their movement towards the desired ideal management style, and this model has resorted to all over the world in order to train managers, and in order to identify different groups of leadership styles.

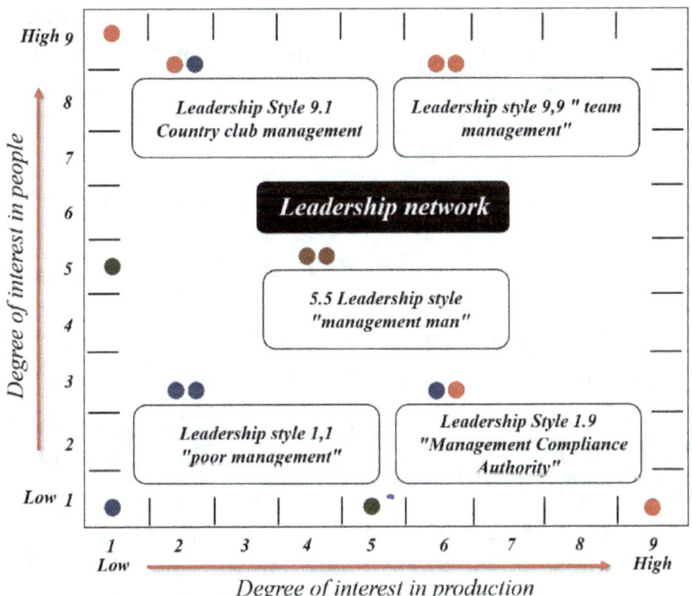

By looking at the shape of the administrative leadership network, we will find that the level of interest in people (employees) will appear on the vertical axis, while the level of interest in production will appear on the horizontal axis of the network, knowing that each axis has a scale ranging from 1 to 9 and that the numbers at the top indicate more attention related to the specified variable, and depending on the degree of managerial concern towards people and production, the manager can take any position on the network.

This administrative network defines 5 leadership styles, and to facilitate reading details of this network, we have allocated three colors to indicate the degree of importance towards one of the variables according to its location on the network, the red color indicates high importance, the light brown color indicates medium importance, while the blue color indicates low importance, the two red arrows indicate the path of transition from low importance to high importance, and the green color occupy the middle position on the axis.

The leadership styles included in this network are:

1- Leadership Style 1,1 "Poor Management"

In the context of this style, it is clear to us that there is a low interest in people, tasks, and production, or in other words, there is no focus on people or production, and the manifestations of leadership are low of "interfering in the affairs of others", and relying on previous practices to maintain the organization's presence in the business world.

2- Leadership Style 9.1 "Management of Country Club"

Through this style, it is clear to us that there is a great interest in people, and a low interest in production, and here managers always strive to try to create an environment for work in which an atmosphere of relaxation, friendliness, and happiness prevails for everyone, however, no one feels disturbed about harnessing the effort required to achieve the goals of the institution.

This management method may be based on the belief that the most important leadership activity is to secure the voluntary cooperation of group members in order to obtain high levels of productivity. Through this method, subordinates provide public reports on high levels of satisfaction to their managers, which can be understood by some who say that these managers are soft and unable to make decisions.

3- Leadership Style 9.1 "Managing Authority Compliance"

In the context of this administrative style, a great interest in production appears, and a low interest in people this administrative style has a directed task related to focusing on the quality of productivity without the desires of subordinates themself, but at the same time their subordinates may feel alienated from them, and as a result, they have to do just enough work to keep themselves out of trouble.

4- Leadership Style 5.5 "Management of the Organizing Man"

This management style is also called "middle-of-the-road management", as it permeates a medium or moderate concern towards production and people, and managers who enjoy working in this administrative style believe in compromise or consensual solutions, and therefore only decisions are taken if approved by subordinates, and these managers can rely upon, they are supportive of the current situation in the organization, but they lack effective leadership, moreover, they may have difficulty in terms of innovation and bringing about the desired change.

5- Leadership Style 9,9 "Team Management"

This management style is characterized by great concern towards both productions as well as employee morale and satisfaction. Team managers believe that concern for people and tasks must be compatible, they are convinced that tasks need to be explained carefully and that decisions must be made by subordinates to achieve a high level of Commitment, according to **Blake and Mouton**, this is the preferred and desirable leadership style.

The managerial network designed by Blake and Mouton, which is widely used for training managers, is a useful tool for identifying and classifying managerial styles, but this tool did not answer the question that says why managers are located in a specific part or another part of this network. In order to determine the reason behind this, one must look at the underlying causes, such as the intrinsic characteristics of the leader or followers, the ability of managers, the organization's environment, and other situational factors that influence how leaders and followers operate.

Chapter four …
Theories of leadership behavior
in organizations

In this chapter, we will get acquainted with each of Fiedler's emergency leadership approaches, and understand the components of the goal path theory. There was no single trait common to all effective leaders, nor was there a single style that was effective in all situations.

Therefore, the researchers began the attempts to identify those factors associated with each case, which affect the effectiveness of a particular style of leadership and began to study different cases in which it is believed that leaders are the product arising from certain situations, and on this basis, many studies were conducted based on the fact that leadership is affected strongly relate to the situations in which it works, and the behaviors of the leader in which they appear.

The theories resulting from this type of study while taken together, constitute the contingent approach to leadership, as it became clear that the situational or contingent approach is of great importance to administrative theory and practice, and that this importance is generated in particular for practicing managers, who must look at the situation when designing an environment to perform tasks.

Speaking about emergency theories of leadership behavior *(theories that deal with emergency situations)*, we will find that they are based on three factors:

1-Requirements for the required task.

2- Organizational culture and policies.

3- The expectations and behavior of colleagues.

As for the most famous situational theories, *"theories that deal with cases that occur in certain circumstances,"* related to leadership behavior, they are:

1- Goal path theory.

2- The Vroom-Yetton model.

3- Fiedler's Emergency Leadership Approach.

4- The Hersey-Blanchard Situational Leadership Model.

Goal path theory

This theory was developed largely by **Robert J. House** and **Terrence R. Mitchell**, the goal-path theory attempts to explain how a leader can help subordinates achieve the goals of an organization, business enterprise, or company by indicating the best possible path to achieve it and removing obstacles that may hinder the achievement of those goals.

This theory indicates that effective leadership will depend, *first, on clearly defined paths to achieve goals for subordinates, and second, on the degree of ability that the leader enjoys in order to improve opportunities for subordinates to achieve their goals*.

In other words, goal path theory proposes setting clear and specific goals for subordinates, the leader must help the subordinates to adopt the best ways to carry out the various tasks, and remove the obstacles they may encounter that may prevent them from achieving the set goals.

Expectations theory is the basis on which the goal-path concept of leadership is built, as this theory indicates that employee motivation depends on aspects of the leader's behavior that affect the performance of the goal-oriented employee and also on the relative attractiveness of the employee from the respective goals, and this theory considers that the individual is the driver behind his awareness of the possibility of achieving the goal through effective job performance, however, the individual must be able to link his efforts to the effectiveness or job performance, which ultimately leads to the achievement of goals.

Expectation's theory consists of three main elements:

1- *Expected performance effort*, which indicates the probability that the employees' efforts will lead to the desired level of performance.

2- *The expected performance according to the results*, refers to the possibility that the successful performance of subordinates will lead to certain results or rewards.

3- *Equivalence between performance and results*, which refers to the perception that subordinates can imagine with regard to results or rewards.

The objective path theory relies on the principle of expectations for motivation, to determine the ways that the leader can take in order to achieve work goals in an easier or more attractive way.

The theory also suggests that there are four styles (behaviors) of leadership that can be used to influence subordinates' perceptions of paths and goals.

1- Effective leadership

Effective leadership behavior includes providing clear guidelines for subordinates, and this leadership describes work methods, develops work schedules, defines performance evaluation criteria, and defines the basis for results or rewards, and it is compatible with the centralization of leadership toward the implementation of tasks.

2- Supportive leadership

Supportive leadership behavior involves creating a pleasant organizational atmosphere in the work environment, and it also involves showing interest in subordinates to become friendlier and more friendly with the leader, a style similar to the concept of relationship-based behavior or considerations.

3- Participatory leadership

Participatory leadership behavior involves the participation of subordinates in decision-making and encouraging proposals from them, which can lead to an increase in their motivation.

4- Advisory leadership

Achievement-oriented leadership behavior involves setting enormous goals in order to help subordinates raise performance to the best possible levels, which generates great confidence from the leader towards his subordinates.

The path-goal theory, unlike Fiedler's theory, indicates that these four styles can be used by the same leader but in different situations.

The attributes of subordinates, such as needs, self-confidence, abilities, and the work environment with its other elements such as tasks, incentive system, and the relationship with co-workers, as shown in the following illustration:

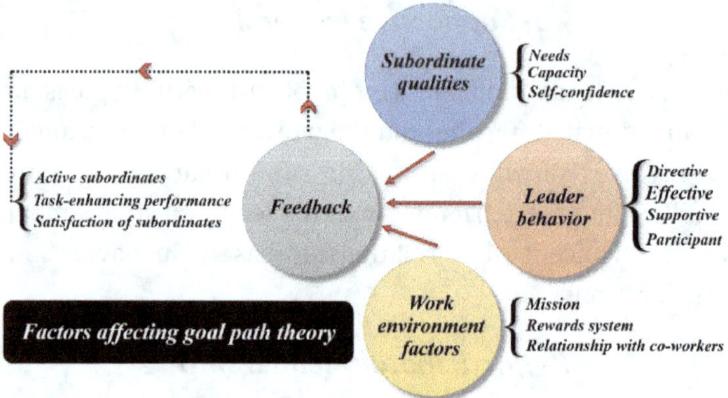

House and Mitchell make two general proposals from the goal-path theory:

A - The behavior of the leader remains acceptable and satisfactory to the subordinates as long as they see that such behavior is either a direct source of satisfaction or a tool for satisfaction in the future.

B- The leader's behavior will remain motivational to the extent that this behavior makes the satisfaction of subordinate's conditional on effective performance, and also indicates that this behavior will complement the environment of subordinates by providing training, guidance, support, rewards, or incentives for effective performance.

In the end, we can point out that the objective path theory will give a great deal of meaning to the practice of management, and we can also say that this model still needs more testing before it can be used as a final approach and guide to administrative work.

Vroom-Yetton model

There is an important issue related to the study of leadership concepts, which is the degree of participation of subordinates in the decision-making process, and based on this hypothesis, two researchers, **Victor Vroom**, and **Philip Yetton** developed a situational leadership model in order to help managers determine when and to what extent to which employees should be involved in solving a specific problem.

Vroom and Yetton's model identified five patterns of leadership behavior based on the degree of subordinate's participation in the decision-making process as follows:

1- The first authoritarian behavior

The features of this behavior seem to be that the leader works to solve the problem facing him or to make the decision on his own only, using the information available to him at the time.

2- The second authoritarian behavior

Through this context, the leader obtains the necessary information from subordinates to solve the existing problem, or perform the required task and then takes the appropriate decision on his own.

3- The first advisory behavior

Through this behavior, the leader discusses the problem with the relevant subordinates individually, obtains from them their ideas and suggestions without bringing them together as a group, and then makes the decision himself, which may or may not reflect the influence of subordinates.

4- The second advisory behavior

This behavior refers to the leader discussing the problem with the relevant subordinates collectively, obtaining from them their ideas and suggestions together as a group, and then making the decision himself, which may or may not reflect the influence of subordinates.

5- Collective behavior

This behavior differs from the previous one, as the leader participates with the subordinates as a group towards solving the problem or performing the required task, where they together create and analyze alternatives and try to reach a consensus on the solution or ways to end the task, and in this case, the leader does not try to obtain adoption of the solution his favorite from the group, he must accept and implement any solution that has the support of the whole group.

Vroom and Yetton have prepared a list of seven questions included in the following table, the answer to which is yes or no, through which the person who will assume the leadership task can choose for himself the appropriate behavior to use towards solving a specific problem or ending a specific task.

The following table shows the cases of the situation that the leader might be exposed to, and the hypothetical questions to be answered.

Situational characteristics	Diagnostic questions
Resolution quality	How important is the technical quality of the decision?
Availability of information	Is there enough information to make a quality decision?
Subject structure (task)	Is the vocabulary of the topic (task) under discussion well structured?
Need for commitment of subordinates	How committed are the subordinates to putting the decision into practice?
Likelihood of commitment	How likely are the subordinates to implement the decision you made as their leader?
Goals matching	Will the subordinates participate towards the implementation of the organizational goals that will be reached to solve the problem?
Conflict between subordinates	Can conflicts arise between subordinates because they give preference to some solutions?

In addition to this list of guiding questions Vroom and Yetton have developed a decision model by matching the decision patterns with the situation according to the answers obtained from asking the seven questions, thus enabling managers to determine the most appropriate style that can be followed by the manager or the leader according to each type of problem by answering these questions, or in other words, the leadership style will become more than appropriate depending on the nature of the problem, or the task.

Recent research conducted by Vroom and other management scholars showed that the decisions that were made in accordance with this model were successful and gained a lot of credibility.

Fiedler's Emergency Leadership Approach

Fred E. Fiedler's approach puts his finger on the starting point of situational leadership research, he and his associates at the **University of Illinois** have proposed the theory of leadership behavior during emergencies, which suggests that people become leaders not just because of their personality traits, but also because of the different situational factors and interactions between leaders and those who follow them.

The basic assumption of Fiedler on which this approach was based is that it is very difficult for managers to work to change the management styles that made them successful in their work, because, in fact, Fiedler believes that most managers are not flexible enough.

Also, trying to change their methods to confront unexpected or volatile situations is ineffective or useless, and since these patterns of managers are relatively inflexible, and since there is no single style that is appropriate for each situation, the group's performance can only be achieved effectively by matching the manager's style with the status or by changing the status to match the manager's style.

Fiedler has identified three critical dimensions of the leadership situation, which will help determine the most effective method for exercising leadership.

A- The power of the position

The level of power of the position as a leader will enable him to rally the group around him and obey his instructions. In the case of managers, this power is what is derived from the authority granted to them by the organizational status of the organization.

According to Fiedler's approach, a leader with great power can recruit followers more easily than those who lack this power.

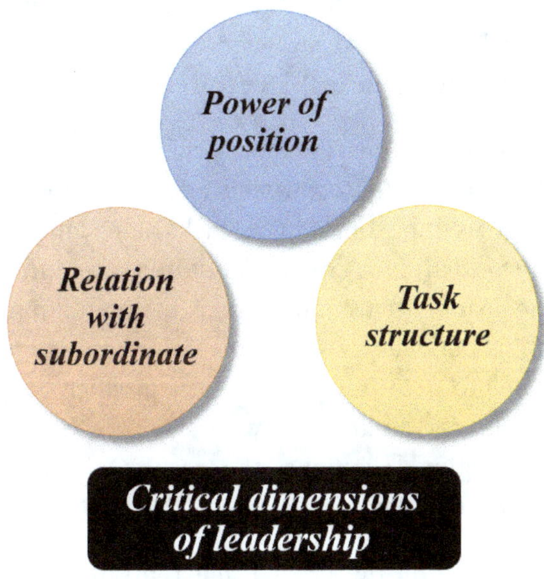

B- Task structure

The meaning task structure refers to the degree to which tasks can be clearly detailed, so that subordinates bear responsibility for their implementation, and therefore when the task structure is clear, it becomes easy to evaluate the quality of employee performance, and define their responsibilities regarding the completion of the task accurately.

C- Relation with subordinates

This title refers to the extent to which subordinate group members believe in the leader's ability, and their willingness to comply with his instructions.

According to Fiedler's approach, the quality of the relationships between the leader and his subordinate member is the most important dimension from the leader's point of view, as the leader may not have the power of the position, or does not have sufficient control and is ignorant of the dimensions of the task structure.

Fiedler believes, he identified two styles of leadership, **the first style is called the task-oriented style**, through which the leader gives importance to the tasks being implemented, and **the second style is called the employee-centric style**, where the leader gives importance to maintaining good relationships between people and gaining more popularity, and in order to determine and measure which of the two styles the leader under study enjoys, Fiedler used an innovative testing technique, the results of which were based on two sources:

1- Scores gained on the Least Preferred Co-worker (LPC) scale **(ratings that group members make to indicate people they least want to work with)**.

Based on this scale, Fiedler found that the leaders who evaluated their subordinates from the workers positively are those who reaped the satisfaction of maintaining good relations among them, while the leaders who evaluated their subordinates from the workers negatively tended to be the ones who direct the implementation of tasks by these subordinates.

Fiedler's model also indicates that the appropriate matching of the leader's style according to this scale, and as identified in the three dimensions of position strength, task structure, and the relationship between the leader and his subordinate member, will lead to effective administrative performance.

For example, in a situation characterized by the absence of appropriate authority, the lack of sufficient strength of the leader, the unclear definition of the task structure, and the absence of the cordial relations that are supposed to exist between the leader and subordinates, all of which would lead to a preference for a leader who is focused on the tasks to be performed.

By contrast, even in favorable situations in which a leader has significant power through position, a well-defined task structure, and good relationships with leaders, Fiedler found that a task-oriented leader would be most effective.

Therefore, Fiedler concluded that an employee-oriented leader would be most effective in moderate situations or situations that lie between these two extremes.

2- Scores gained on the "Assumed Similarity Between Opposites" - "ASO" scale (an assessment that is based on determining the degree of similarity among group members by leaders), and this scale is based on the assumption that people work better with those whom they could have some kind of relationship.

Hersey and Blanchard model

The Leadership Behavior Model of **Paul Hersey** and **Kenneth H. Blanchard** is one of the most important approaches to what is called the situational or contingent leadership approach, and this approach is based on the premise that leaders need to change their behavior depending on a major situational factor, such as the willingness of subordinates to follow them to do the task.

Hersey and Blanchard have defined the concept of readiness as the desire for achievement, the willingness to accept responsibility, the ability for the relevant task, experience, and skill, or in other words, it refers to the willingness and ability of subordinates to deal with a particular task.

The common belief of Hersey and Blanchard indicates that the relationship between the leader and a subordinate group moves through four stages that govern the development of these subordinates over time, and therefore leaders need to change their leadership style.

Hersey and Blanchard have designed a table that shows the basics that govern their leadership model, and from this table, we can notice that what is called **task behavior** refers to the extent to which the leader has to provide the required direction to the individual or group, and this includes telling people what needs to be done, when to do it, how to do it, and who is responsible for doing it.

Relationship behavior	Task behavior	Leader's behavior
Low	High	*In the initial stage of "readiness," managers must clearly articulate duties and responsibilities to the group, as employees need to be directed in their tasks*
High	High	*Over time the subordinates will learn to perform their tasks but the leaders still need to provide the required direction to them*
High	Low	*Subordinates become more capable of achieving, and the search process begins vigorously toward assuming responsibility. Leaders do not need the direction process as it was in the previous time, but they must be supportive and their considerations are of a high level.*
Low	Low	*Subordinates become more experienced and confident, leaders can reduce the dose of support and encouragement, and subordinates no longer need direction, as they can make decisions on their own*

As for what is called **relationship behavior**, it refers to the degree of participation in two directions through communication (between the leader and the group), and this includes listening, providing facilities, and supporting behaviors.

In the first stage of "readiness", (the readiness of subordinates for the task), the duties and responsibilities of the relevant group must be clarified with the utmost precision, and this matter is considered appropriate because the employees must need instructions to carry out their tasks, and they must also be aware of the rules of conducting work in the organization, business institution, or the entity, and its procedures, and it would be inappropriate to resort to participatory behavior at this stage, given that subordinates still need to understand the nature and how the organization, or business institution, or the entity works towards carrying out the relevant task.

Distributed Leadership

Leadership has fascinated many researchers and has been widely studied in universities and research institutes. However, to this day there is no generally accepted approach to leadership behaviors, even during World War II of the last century, leadership behaviors were determined by the personality traits of the leader.

The prevailing belief has always been that leaders are born and not made, and on the other hand, there was an approach indicating that leadership is a *"set of behaviors and procedures"* that can be learned, and another approach appeared indicating that what is called *"situational or emergency leadership"*, which emphasizes that leadership styles must depend on the relevant situation.

According to this last approach, we can say that there is no specific leadership style that can be effective in all cases, and therefore the leader must resort to using the appropriate leadership style according to each case, this leads us to another new approach that refers to what is called **"distributed leadership."**, as a modern approach that has become popular in our world today, which is based on the following assumptions:

• Let it be understood that leadership is based on organizations and not on individuals.

• Individuals, groups, and organizations tend to be more effective when leadership is distributed.

• Individuals have the ability to lead if they are provided with the appropriate training and support required.

• The powers and functions of the leader must be shared, as they are not limited to a specific person only, or to a group of elites.

• Let it be understood that leadership is not just a set of independent characteristics enjoyed by the leader, but it must be seen as a process that includes specific steps.

Through this approach, we can discover three different and complementary types of leadership styles, and each of these styles of leadership requires a different role, a different mentality, and a different time scale. At the leadership level of senior management in organizations, bodies, business institutions, or companies, there will be an urgent need for a **"vision"** that leads to framing the strategies and goals.

This visionary element of leadership must not only take into account organizational strategies, but must also respond to the changes that may occur, and others that are expected to occur, which requires this type of relevant leadership to show insight and farsightedness.

It follows from this vision that what is called *"integrative leadership"*, through which leaders integrate each of the institutional vision, values, strategy, systems development, and processes necessary to meet operational needs, and the matter does not stop there, rather, the leaders must solve any problems that may exist between the units of the entity.

Through this method, leaders should be able to see beyond the current situation, that is, they should have the ability to foresee the future, and they should have an open mindset that includes a broader field than just the space in which the organization, body, or institution or the company resides.

As for the team level of subordinates or the level of a project, there will also be an urgent need to fill the role of leadership, in order to complete this project or achieve results efficiently and effectively, knowing that the time scale is always short, which requires the leader to focus on the project and make an effort to delight customers or consumers.

These types of leadership behaviors must require different abilities, furthermore, different organizational contexts require different skills, for example, leadership in a marketing situation requires different skills than in a financing situation.

Different leadership situations also require different leadership styles, for example, some cases may require an urgent or expedited decision, while others require consultation with different members of the relevant entity.

Distributed leadership requires a strong communication system through which leaders at different levels can communicate with each other, knowing that the key to successful distributed leadership is ensuring freedom of dealing and action. It should be allowed for every leader to work under the umbrella of the entity, and over time the subordinates will learn how to accomplish the tasks successfully, and despite that, it is still necessary for the leader to always adopt direction as needed, as the feedback of the new employees are almost and certainly not fully familiar with the way the entity operates.

In addition, leaders must get to know their subordinates well, in order to work to raise the pace of mutual trust, because this is the stage that needs to increase the behavior of relationships, which accelerates the birth of the next stage, the stage in which subordinates become more capable, and their activism towards seeking greater responsibility is evident.

Within this method and when the subordinates reach this stage, the leader is not required to be directed to carry out the tasks as was before, but he must still be supportive and provide the required care so that this enables the subordinates to assume greater responsibilities, and the more these subordinates enjoy with more experience and confidence, the less support and encouragement from the leader.

In the last stage of the distributed leadership style, the leader's direction to subordinates can be completely dispensed with, because they will be able to make decisions themselves.

Hersey and Blanchard model believes that the situational leadership style must be effective and flexible, in order to determine the combination of the most appropriate leadership style in a specific context, which will be relied upon, and the motivation, level of experience of subordinates and their abilities must be evaluated, and all of this must be re-evaluated with a change in context.

According to them, if the chosen leadership style is appropriate, it will not only motivate subordinates but will also help them develop their careers, so a leader who wants to help his team to advance and increase their level of confidence in what they are doing, he must change his leadership style according to their needs.

When a leader is flexible in his leadership style, in this case, he will be effective in a variety of leadership situations, but on the other hand, if he is relatively inflexible in his leadership style, he can be effective only in those situations that suit his preferred style of leadership as a result, some effort must be made in order to modify some of the characteristics of the situation to suit the style of this leader.

We can say today that there is a growing number of situational theories related to leadership styles and that each approach to these theories adds a piece of insight toward your understanding of leadership, and although Fiedler's theory has the largest research base, as it was formulated and prepared early, it seems that Vroom and Yetton's theory offers promising properties in the training of managers.

The following table contains a brief explanation of comparisons and preferences related to the four leadership theories that emphasize the importance of situational variables, and on which they depend:

• Measuring leader behavior in terms of selection rate.

• Measuring applications in terms of earned value for managers.

• Measuring the research base in terms of the number of studies supporting the theory.

Theories				
Comparison	**Hersey-Blanchard**	**Vroom-Yetton**	**Goal path**	**Fiedler**
The topic	*Successful leaders adapt their styles to the demands of the situation*	*Successful leadership style identifies the situation, the leader can learn to recognize the requirements of the situation and how to adapt his style to meet these requirements*	*Successful leaders are the ones who increase the motivation of subordinates by drawing and clarifying the paths of effective performance*	*Not the best. A leader's success is determined by the interaction between the environment and his or her subjective variables (personality)*
Leader behavior	*Tends to complete tasks and direct the relationship*	*Authoritarian and inclined to share*	*Tends to direct towards achievement*	*Tends to direct the relationship or task*
search base	*Low but generally supportive*	*Low but increasing, generally supportive*	*Medium to low, generally supportive*	*Expansive and includes many fields such as industry and education, marred by some contradictory results*
Applications	*Medium, but increasing*	*High and leaders can train on its methods*	*Medium*	*Medium to low is generally difficult for leaders to learn*

Transformational leadership theory

The business world has recently realized that managers in different entities will not necessarily become leaders, and according to one point of view, managers do things right, but it may require leaders to have the ability to innovate and do things right, and leaders must also work to inspire their subordinates to exhaust extraordinary levels of effort.

German Sociologist Max Weber introduced the concept of charisma (attraction) during the discussions on leadership, where he considered charisma an adaptation of the theological concept of possessing divine grace, and that leaders who possess charisma have a great influence on their followers, as they are attracted to the personality of the leader with what it metaphorically carries. His magnetism, oratorical skills, and exceptional ability to respond to crises.

James MacGregor Burns, a pioneer in the study of leadership, discussed the concept of (a hero), and according to Burns, heroic leadership can be seen in leaders who inspired their followers and were able to transform their orientations.

While leadership expert ***Bernard M. Bass*** extends what is called Burns' view, describing a transformational leader as someone who motivates people to perform beyond normal expectations by inspiring them to focus on broader tasks beyond their immediate self-interest and to focus on higher core goals (such as achievement and self-fulfillment), instead of other, lower goals (such as safety and security), and to have confidence in their abilities to achieve the exceptional tasks expressed by the leader, and according to him, transformational leadership exhibits the following attributes:

1- Charismatic leadership.

2- Individual considerations.

3- Intellectual stimulation ***(such as presenting new ideas to motivate followers, encouraging them to look at problems from multiple angles, and promoting creative***

breakthroughs for obstacles that seemed insurmountable).

The insight offered by Burns suggests that leaders are able to motivate, effect transformation, and use the values, beliefs, and needs of their followers to get things done and that leaders who do this through rapid change or withstanding crisis are transformational leaders.

Other approaches to leadership such as the behavioral or situational approach usually focus on what is termed transactional leadership. Leaders who are receptive to their followers as transformational leaders are perceived as more charismatic and intellectually stimulating than transactional leaders.

One of the main differences between the transactional leader and the transformational leader is that the transactional leader motivates his subordinates towards performing to be at the expected levels, whereas the transformational leader motivates his subordinates to perform beyond normal expectations.

Here, we must acknowledge that transformational leadership is not a substitute for transactional leadership, as it is considered a complementary element of leadership with an additional effect represented in performance that exceeds expectations, and the reason for this is that even the most successful transformational leaders need transactional skills, as well as effective management of daily events, that form the basis for broader missions.

However, there is still a potential area of concern regarding the discussion of more information about the characteristics of transformational leadership, which is that the discussion and interpretations are beginning to resemble the approach of early features of leadership theory.

Finally, seeking what constitutes divine grace, charisma, and ability to influence is like examining human traits such as intelligence, self-confidence, and physical traits to determine what makes for success.

Chapter five ...
Motivations of subordinates in organizations

With any type of economic and non-economic entity, the manager must know what motivates the workers under his command in order to make each one of them perform the best according to his ability, knowing that it is not easy to deal with the workers because they respond in different ways towards their work and towards the organizational practices within these entities.

Motivation is a psychological characteristic of a person, which has an impact on the degree of commitment of the individual towards his work, or in other words, it is a group of forces that move the individual towards achieving a specific goal, and it deals with how to activate the behavior of workers, how it is directed and how it continues, so the challenge facing managers is limited to how to direct the energy and behavior of employees towards achieving the objectives of the relevant entity.

Factors affecting work incentives include both individual differences and organizational practices. Individuals differ in their personal needs, values, behaviors, interests, and abilities. As for organizational practices that affect motivation, they include rules, policies, administrative practices, and reward systems.

To motivate employees, managers must consider how these factors affect them personally, and their job or professional performance.

Define and the concept of motivation

According to **Stephen P. Robbins**, motivation is the desire to make high levels of effort towards organizational goals, conditioned on the ability of effort to meet some individual needs, while **Fred Luthans** sees motivation as a process that begins when a deficiency appears in the physiology of the individual, or the need to activate the behavior or the desire that aims to achieve a specific goal or motive, *so the three main elements in the mentioned definitions are needs, desire, and goals*.

Needs create the desire to achieve goals, this is the basic process of motivation, which can be seen in the following illustration:

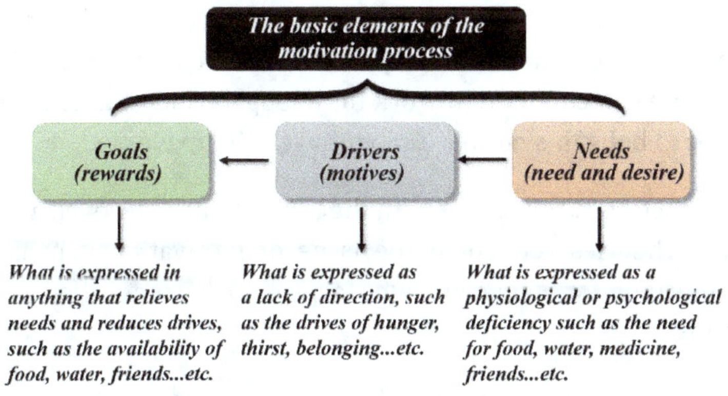

The need is the origin of any motivational behavior, and it refers to the feeling of deprivation of the psychological or well-being of a person, and the need appears in individuals to varying degrees, and when the individual feels the need, the desire will lead him towards meeting that need.

If desires are the engine towards achieving goals and directed towards the completion of work will provide an active incentive towards achieving goals or obtaining rewards, this leads us, in the end, to recognize that each of the incentives or goals are the tools used to get people to follow the required course of action and that once the desired goal is achieved, the physiological or psychological balance is restored and the desires cease.

Classification of motivation theories

In this chapter, we will explain each of the following, the hierarchy of needs according to **Abraham H. Maslow**, and also the limitations of Maslow's model.

Many theories relating to needs have been developed by behavioral scientists regarding how managements in different entities motivate workers. These theories help managers to understand why an individual chooses to work, why he can continue to work for a long period of time, and how to boost his morale and motivate him to work.

Production is consistent with the highest possible level, and thus theories related to the issue of motivation become important for managers who aspire to become effective leaders.

In this context, we can classify motivation theories into two categories:

• Theories of content or need.

• Theories of the stimulus process (treatment).

Motivation theories are based on the needs that work to determine the motives that direct individual behavior, and therefore the theories of need emphasize that the way we behave depends entirely on our own needs that we are trying to reach, so they accurately determine what motivate the individual towards something, and thus logically, it determines the content of the individual's needs, and therefore these theories are called *(content theories)*.

There are many other theories concerned with the mechanisms of motivation, and these theories are referred to as motivational *(processing)* theories of process.

From the following table, we can identify what each of the content theories and process theories can do towards motivating workers.

Topic	Characteristics	Theories	Managers behaviors
Content	*Giving attention to factors that trigger, initiate or initiate the motivational behavior*	*The need for each of the theory of hierarchy, the theory of two factors, and the theory of existence, interdependence and growth*	*Provide motivation to individuals by meeting financial needs, job status and achievement at work*
Action	*Giving attention not only toward factors that elicit behavior, but also with task management, direction, or choice of behavioral patterns*	*The need for both expectations theory and justice theory*	*Provide motivation depending on the individual's perception of work input, performance requirements and reward system*

Maslow's hierarchy of needs theory

This theory is one of the most common explanations for human motivation, which was developed by the psychologist, Abraham Maslow, and received great acclaim during the early 1960s, where this theory indicates that human needs form a hierarchy of five levels: *physiological needs, safety and security needs, social needs (love and belonging), self-esteem needs, and self-actualization needs, as shown in the following illustration.*

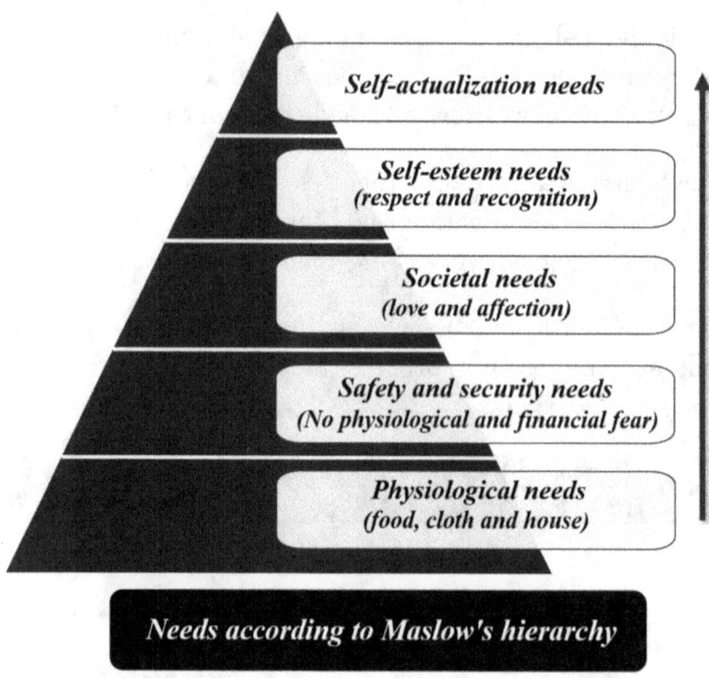

1- Physiological needs

Physiological needs are the basic needs of a person; such as food, clothing, shelter ... etc., and for this, the various entities must allocate appropriate and sufficient wages for their workers in order to achieve these needs, and according to Maslow's theory, that until these needs are met to the degree necessary to maintain life, the stimulus process will remain valid, while achieving any other secondary needs will not trigger the individual's motivation process, moreover, once these basic needs are met, the motivation process will end.

2- The need for safety and security

Once the physiological needs of the individual are met, the individual's consideration will be directed towards meeting his needs of safety and security, which refer to his need for freedom from fear of physical, psychological, or financial harm, and once the individual feels that his need for security has been fulfilled to a reasonable extent, his consideration will automatically direct to the development of his relationships with the others.

3- Social needs

This type of need is also called affiliation needs or the need to feel loved, and it includes the individual's desire to join others and their acceptance of him, and therefore we will find that managers of successful entities work to meet these needs for their subordinates, by allowing social interaction among them through planning suitable for distributing offices, providing them with decoration that stimulates the soul to work, allocating some time from the daily work time for what is called coffee breaks, providing them with lunch, and preparing facilities for entertainment .... etc.

4- Self-esteem needs

This level represents the higher needs of human beings, and they include the desire to obtain a positive self-image, respect, and recognition of others. Successful entities understand well the extent of the impact of these needs on certain types of subordinates, so these entities seek to meet these needs through some mechanisms.

Either by rewarding the employee with higher wages, or promotion, or providing him with a well-furnished office, or providing him with a car, or a personal assistant and other benefits such as share options, club membership, etc., of course, such measures (some or all of them) will achieve the need for self-esteem that the individual aspires to in the entity.

5- *Self-actualization needs*

This type of need occupies the top of the hierarchy of Maslow's theory, as the concept of these needs refers to the individual's need to achieve his full potential through continuous development and self-development processes.

These needs are characterized by the individual's interest in issues such as the freedom to express his creativity and the translation of innovative ideas into reality, pursue knowledge, and develop his talents in directions that may be unknown

Most management experts feel that the need for self-actualization can be met by allowing subordinates to participate in decision-making and giving them the ability to shape their job assignments.

Maslow's theory indicates that the importance of lower needs (physiological, safety, security, and social needs) decreases as an individual progresses upward through the hierarchy of needs.

This is based on the fact that when an individual joins a job, he does so in order to meet his basic physiological needs of food, clothing, and shelter, and once these needs are met, he seeks job security to meet his safety needs. Here, he may join a social organization or a club to meet his social needs, and once his social needs are met, his goal becomes to achieve higher levels of needs such as esteem and self-realization.

Limitations of Maslow's Theory

Many research studies have been conducted on the theory of the hierarchy of needs in organizations, and these studies revealed that human needs do not always appear in a hierarchical manner, as the opposite of Maslow's hierarchy can be seen represented by the artist who is looking for a living in his attempt to fulfill his needs and for self-realization despite That his physiological and security needs are not being met.

Similarly, Maslow's theory does not explain how a person prioritizes needs at a certain level of the hierarchy. For example, a person may experience more than one physiological need such as hunger, thirst, and shelter, and that any of these needs will be satisfied first.

About a decade after the publication of his original paper, Maslow tried to clarify his position by saying that it was a matter of satisfaction that the fulfillment of the need for the self-esteem of individuals who are motivated for self-development could increase rather than decrease the pursuit of the need for self-actualization, and in later related perceptions, Maslow recognized the occasional possibility of some setbacks towards the hierarchy of needs.

Chapter six…
Leadership role and the
development of organizations

Leadership is the backing and support provided by the leader-manager to subordinates by involving them in all leadership operations based on the principle of support. Successful leadership is the one that represents the role model in administrative work, and it is the ability of the leader to know the most appropriate circumstances and times in which the foundations and principles of leadership can be applied, and an example of that is achieving a balance between individual needs and business needs.

Leadership means the vision necessary for the administrative leader regarding the future of the organization or department that he works to lead and then work after that to transform this vision into reality, with the need for the presence, support, and backup of others and not to coerce or force them to work.

The real leadership is the one that tries to lead others instead of resorting to blaming them, and the participation of others in all stages of implementation, as it is an art that can be learned, trained, and applied in reality. It is just thinking about what those in power do, reflecting the functional approach.

If leadership is the ability to get someone to do something they would not otherwise do, leadership has many different definitions. However, the differences revolve around four areas. The empirical models of leadership are common elements between different leadership styles, and we will review these elements in the following context:

1- Functional leadership

This type of leadership refers to linking leadership to a spatial location, such as various entities like profit and non-profit organizations. Leadership is the activity practiced by a person who occupies a functional position at the top of a hierarchy that allows him to direct the workers under his umbrella and lead them to achieve the goals of the entity that he represents.

It is also how we usually look at the bosses who sit at the top of the hierarchy, and that leadership may also appear in the form of legitimizing forbidden behaviors, as this dimension is based on status and leadership differs here depending on the extent to which it is formally or informally organized, and the extent to which it is established horizontally or vertically. Leadership in positions of responsibility involves some degree of centralization toward resources and authority.

2- Personal leadership

People-based leadership defines an approach to the leader's core attributes, competencies, or behaviors that are compatible with how organizations achieve their goals so that such an approach is related to the human relationship between the leader and his subordinates, and

3- Feedback-based leadership

It is the leadership that follows the approach based on the feedback or results that are reached depending on the role of the leader and what he achieved in terms of goals and objectives for the business organization or the related entity, and this type of leadership includes what the organization seeks towards development and also changes the style of leadership in relation to the goals that have been achieved, and goals guaranteed to be achieved.

4- Operations leadership

It is the type of leadership based on the implementation of operations, and it is considered one of the strategic roles of leader-manager, as he must have the ability to persuade and influence others, and he has the characteristics and skills that enable him to perform the leadership role effectively and efficiently, whether inside or outside the work environment and accomplish these tasks.

The leader is highly skilled, in planning, organizing, coordinating, and making decisions, and he has the psychological skills related to understanding the positive and negative nature of leadership, which represents the main key to ensuring the fulfillment of leadership requirements.

Among the most important characteristics of a successful leader-manager is honesty, emotional stability, consultation with others, showing strength, acumen, and foresight when making decisions, defining the goal to be achieved accurately, harnessing his energy in order to achieve the goal and a balance between focus and motivation, and focus is the vision or the general goal, and directs all efforts towards activity, while motivation is the ability to maintain energy and enthusiasm.

The leader must also have what we can call human intelligence, that is, the ability of the leader-manager to understand the feelings and emotions of his workers, the ability to control this human intelligence, and work to instill confidence between him and his workers in order to motivate them towards achieving the goals of the organization.

Where this comes through the realization represented by discovering the emotional state of others, identifying the ideas associated with them, and the emotional maturity represented by the ability of the administrative leader to control his feelings towards others, and adapting to difficult situations in a way that leads to achieving full confidence, and balancing between the elements of commitment and empowerment In order to adhere to standards and help others to reach the highest levels of performance.

Among the characteristics of the successful leader-manager is resorting to the creative thinking method, through his ability to present strategies, creative ideas, and the right choice among them to ensure the achievement of the goals of the organization efficiently and effectively, and he must also have the ability to link all processes, events, and systems that it affects the performance of the organization by examining all available alternatives and paying attention to the processes that increase the ability to seize learning opportunities and improve the level of performance.

Chapter seven …
Organizational culture and leadership styles

One of the irrefutable facts is the constant pursuit of psychology through various related studies towards discovering and understanding how members of different cultures interact with each other, and with the time passing, leadership has evolved across those cultures as a tool for understanding the characteristics of leaders-managers in order to confront the complexities of this era, the era of globalization, as the multinational organizations are today in deep need of leaders-managers who can adapt to different environments quickly, and work with partners and employees of other cultures, in order to establish the principle saying that a successful manager in one country must be successful in another country.

These studies involve looking at the social construction of various organizations or other entities, in order to discover contradictions in organizational behavior, that is, in the social relations between the members of these organizations and entities, given that the organization today has become a testing ground for the embodiment of economic and administrative expertise that qualifies to assume the positions of managers and leaders.

Those experiences from which it derives the ability to act, and to integrate internally with the workers, knowing that their competence is determined according to their abilities to produce a culture that qualifies them towards harmony, balance, and the mobilization of qualified and integrable human resources.

Among what must be considered in relation to leadership is what tacit leadership theory emphasizes that people's basic assumptions, stereotypes, beliefs, and schemes influence the extent to which they view a person in terms of acceptance or rejection as a good person or not because people across cultures they tend to hold multiple implicit beliefs, schemas, and stereotypes, and therefore it will be natural for their core beliefs to vary, which makes the characteristics of a good leader different due to different cultures.

The so-called Hofstede dimensions (Gerard Hendrik Hofstede) of culture are considered one of the prominent and influential studies regarding leadership in the world of globalization. This study revealed the similarities and differences between different cultures around the world.

At the same time, the study emphasized the necessity of open-mindedness in order to identify the differences in other cultures and work to understand them well.

In this study, Hofstede resorted to identifying six dimensions of culture in order to make the required comparison between the different cultures of the world, in order to give leaders a good and documented understanding of how to adjust their leadership styles for individuals and businesses.

These dimensions included:

Power distance index (PDI), Individualism vs. collectivism (IDV), Uncertainty avoidance (UAI), Masculinity vs. femininity (MAS), Long-term orientation vs. short-term orientation (LTO), and Indulgence vs. restraint (IND).

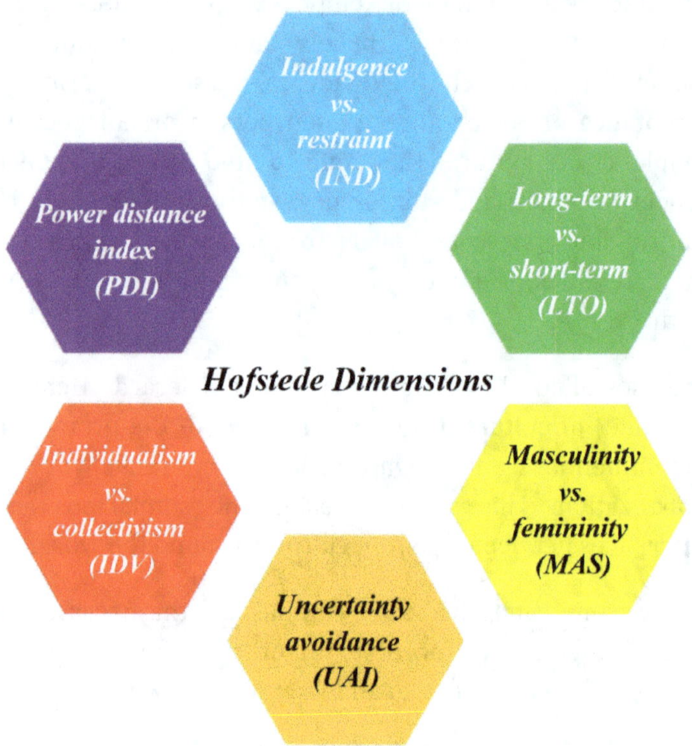

Leadership, as we mentioned earlier, is what the manager or individual possesses of the ability to influence others to motivate and encourage them to accomplish a set of desired goals for the organization or entity, and it can also be described as a set of activities practiced by the administrative leader in all areas that require decision-making and implementation, thus issuing orders to subordinates.

Leadership is represented by influencing subordinates in general and directing their behavior in the line with the goals and interests of the organization. Leadership also works hard to coordinate the efforts of workers to provide what is best for them. So that they can provide the best for the organization or entity in order to reach and achieve the desired results.

Leadership is considered the link between the perceptions of the organization and its employees, and it plays an important role in harnessing the efforts of employees in the required direction in line with the desired goals.

Leadership also plays a major role in controlling the problems facing the workflow and finding the necessary solutions to them and contributing to training individuals and providing them with care, development, and motivation, in order to improve and develop their human and practical skills.

Organizational culture in different organizations and entities

Organizational culture is the basics of the system that brings together the ideas, customs, traditions, and ways of thinking of the members of the organization or entity with each other, and they participate in them, which would affect their behavior and control their experiences, and which in turn affect the productivity and efficiency of the organization or entity.

Organizational culture includes ways to organize the work of subordinates, the nature of their leadership, their rewards and evaluation systems, as well as the vocabulary of the daily work wheel, oversight and control, strategies and goals to be achieved...etc.

The importance of organizational culture lies in the formation of patterns of behavior and relationships that must be followed by members of the same organization, whether they are employees or managers, raising the organization's ability to change and cope with developments that occur in the organization around it, and determining the functional behavior expected of the individuals working in the organization, and determining the nature of their relationships with each other and their relationships with customers, determining the way employees dress (uniform) and the style of language they speak, and maintaining the stability of the organization.

Organizational culture is an auxiliary and supportive element for the management of the organization and helps it achieve its aspirations and goals, obtain innovation in work and avoid routine, directing individuals working in the same organization, work to organize their work, and attract ambitious, creative and required workers to achieve the goals of the organization.

Types of organizational leadership cultures in organizations and entities

According to recent studies related to business administration, it was possible to identify six types of organizational cultures in various organizations and other entities. These cultures include mission culture, creativity culture, role culture, bureaucratic culture, operations culture, and supportive culture.

Task culture

It is the culture in which the focus is on work results and the extent to which working individuals use the resources available in the organization or the entity to achieve the best results.

Innovative culture

It is the culture that provides a work environment that helps achieve creativity, and its members are usually characterized by daring in making their decisions.

Role culture

The focus of this culture is limited to the specializations of individuals working in the organization or entity and their roles, and this culture ensures continuity and job stability.

Bureaucratic Culture

It is the culture in which most of the authorities and responsibilities that rest with the members of the organization or entity are determined, and in which authority is hierarchical and based on commitment.

Process culture

It is the culture in which attention is paid to the way work is done and not to its results, and the successful individual in it is usually the one who protects himself and is organized and accurate in his work.

Supportive culture

It is the culture in which the focus is on the human aspect, and the cooperative atmosphere prevails in the organization or entity among the workers.

Determinants of organizational leadership culture

Research and studies refer to the multiplicity of determinants of the culture of organizational leadership in different organizations and entities, as the most prominent of these determinants are the work environment of the organization or entity, size, objectives, prevailing technology, nature and quality of employees, type of ownership, and date of starting of work.

The environment refers to the way the organization or entity deals with the elements of its internal or external environment, whether they are employees, suppliers, or competitors, that environment affects the way resources and activities are organized and the formation of its culture.

The difference in the size of the organization or entity does not necessarily affect its organization, but what affects is the way the organization is managed and the styles of behaving in different situations, which in turn are affected by this size.

As for the goals, the organizational culture is usually affected by these goals that the organization strives to achieve. For example, if the organization wants to raise the level of customer service, it must focus its organizational culture on consolidating the values associated with customer and employee relations.

Organizations and entities specializing in the use of technology are based on values related to technical skills in their organizational culture, while service organizations are based on customer service and personal skills in their organizational culture.

Individuals have a major role in defining organizational culture, as management cannot impose a culture that the organization or entity's members do not believe in, just as individuals cannot prefer a specific organizational culture that management does not want.

The history of the development of the organization or entity, and the quality of leadership are what reflect its culture.

The type of ownership also plays a major role in determining the organizational culture, whether this ownership is public or private, and whether it is local or international.

In fact, it was found that the more successful and stronger the organizational leadership culture is, the more it can create a business atmosphere that is characterized by discipline and managing various businesses easily and smoothly. It is not possible to disagree with the fact that the ability of the leaders of the organization towards achieving the optimal investment is based on the diversity and multiplicity of cultures that have an impact on contributing to the generation of thought that creates creativity, consequently, this will lead to providing appropriate solutions to many of the dilemmas left behind by the bureaucracy. As a result, a broad ground will emerge in which the visions and fruits of cooperation will be embodied.

Organizational leadership will create a fertile environment that allows the growth and distinction of a strong organizational culture that has a positive impact on the benefit of the organization in order to integrate its goals with the goals of its employees and the goals of the customers for whom it was established.

There is no doubt that open culture leadership will lead to the establishment of new principles and practices in the organization or entity, taken from the experiences of practices of other sectors and organizations that are suitable for application in the same organizational field. It has become evident that the new directions taken by the leadership philosophy to create a kind of distinction in its organizational culture, by moving towards the style of the appropriate private sector practices.

This can be done by encouraging and adopting the idea of partnership and development to achieve the principle of innovation and the development of organizational competencies, which facilitates the benefit from the qualitative methodology and the adoption of electronic applications in order to form a distinguished methodology that contributes to making part of effective solutions to mitigate or get rid of the bad bureaucracy. This allows as well a reconsideration of the method and practice of centralization and decentralization to reflect the principle of cooperation in a more integrated manner to achieve better results.

Recent studies related to organizational behavior have unanimously agreed that organizational culture is an essential element in the organization's system or entity, with its impact on workers and operations, including values, ethics, habits, ideas, and policies that direct the behavior of individuals in which they work, hence, this culture influences through them the efficiency and effectiveness of the organization or entity.

Accordingly, the organizational culture will influence and be affected by the culture of leaders, and therefore they must understand its dimensions and components as the environmental medium in which organizations and various entities live, which affects the type of behavior with which they interact with others or with their employees.

This matter must depend on the wisdom of the organizational leadership to make its concern to create a supportive and common culture matching the culture of employees and the culture of operations that focuses on hard work and performance required to achieve the common goals of the organization or entity, employees, and customers, on which the ability to judge the success of the performance of organizations or entities depends.

References

*- Essentials of Management - Harold Koontz, Heinz Weihrich, McGraw-Hill, 1990.

*- Narayana Murthy and the Legend of Infosys, Diamond Pocket Books Pvt Ltd, Oct, 2016.

*- Leadership: Abstracts and bibliography. 1904 to 1974, Ralph M. Stogdill, College of Administrative Science, Columbus, Ohio, Monograph, 1977.

*- Principles of Topological Psychology, Kurt Lewin, Martino Fine Books, 2015.

*- How to Choose a Leadership Pattern, Robert Tannenbaum, Warren H. Schmidt, Harvard Business School Publishing Corporation, 2008.

*- Likert's System 4 - Organizational Behavior for Professional Managers, Rensis Likert, Amacom, 1972.

* -The Managerial Grid, Robert Rogers Blake, Jane Srygley Mouton, Gulf Pub., 1994.

*- A Theory of Leadership Effectiveness, Fred Edward Fiedler, McGraw-Hill, 1967.

*- Path Goal Theory of Leadership, Robert J. House, Terence R. Mitchell, Faculty of Management Studies, University of Toronto, 1975.

*- Leadership and Decision-Making, Victor H. Vroom, Philip W. Yetton, University of Pittsburg Press, 1973.

*- Management of Organizational Behavior: Utilizing Human Resources, Paul Hersey, Kenneth H. Blanchard, Prentice-Hall on India Private Limited, 1974.

*- Charisma, Bureaucracy, Max Weber, General Books LLC, 2010.

*- Leadership, James MacGregor Burns, Open Road Media, 2012.

*- Leadership and Performance Beyond Expectations, Bernard M. Bass, Free Press, 1985.

*- Organizational Behavior, Fred Luthans, McGraw-Hill Singapore, 1989.

*- Organizational Behavior: Concept Controversies and Applications,, Stephen P. Robbins, Prentice-Hall, Englewood Cliffs, N.J., 1989.

*- A Theory of Human Motivation, Abraham H. Maslow, Simon and Schuster, 2013.

www.ingramcontent.com/pod-product-compliance
Lightning Source LLC
Chambersburg PA
CBHW061324250726
48657CB00016B/777